THE YOKE'S ON US

CURIOSITY, PRACTICE, AND TRACING THE THREAD

ANNE JABLONSKI

CONTENTS

For Carie Garrett

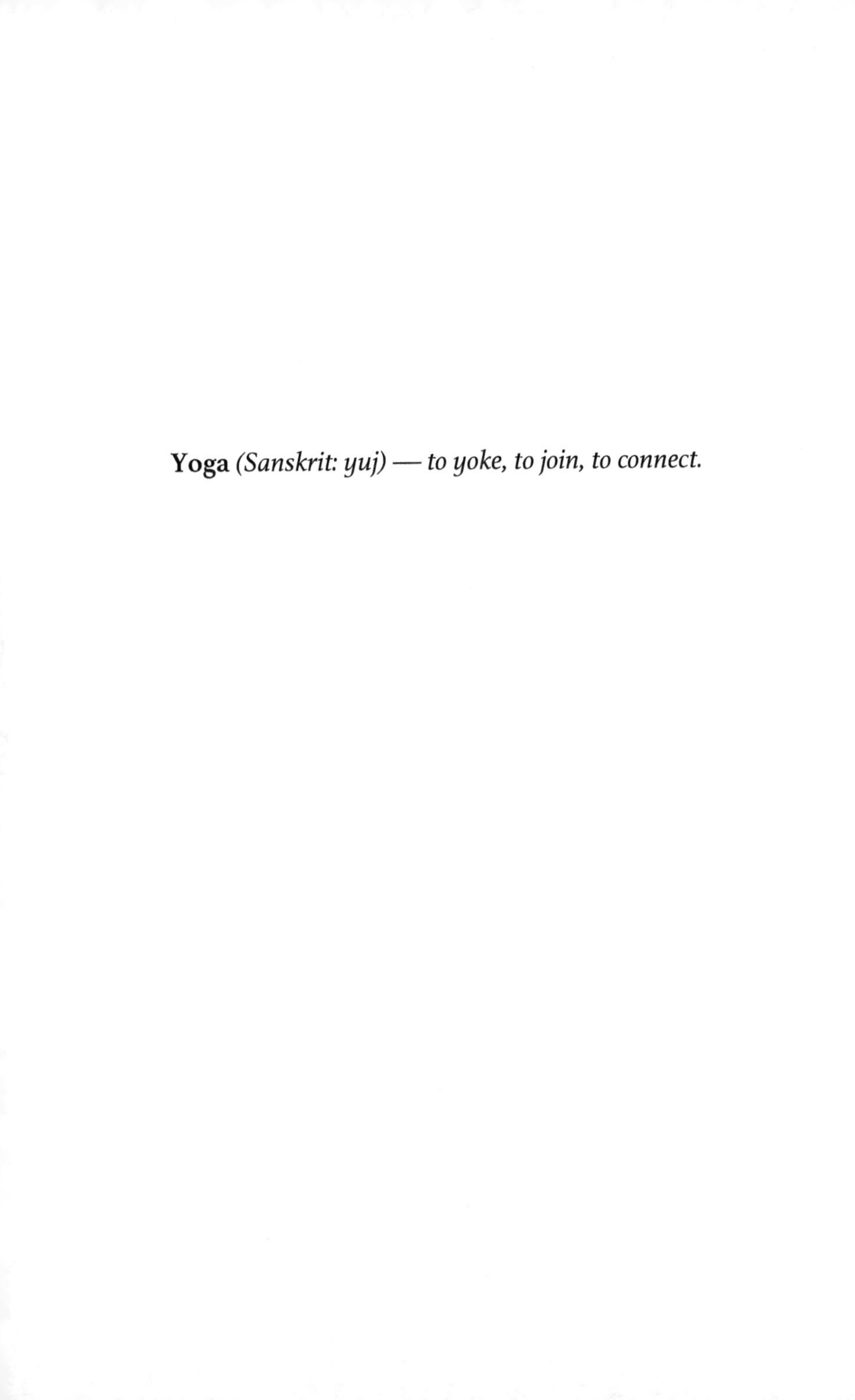

Yoga *(Sanskrit: yuj) — to yoke, to join, to connect.*

AUTHOR'S NOTE

Let's begin with full disclosure: I didn't write this little book because I reached enlightenment, clarity, or even basic consistency. I wrote it because I kept uncovering insights the way an amateur sleuth finds clues: by accident, often while looking for something else.

If you've read the opening chapter, you already know this book began the way many of my real-life reckonings do: with curiosity rising, confusion swirling, identity shifting at the seams, timing refusing to cooperate, and the slow, liberating realization that coming of age may not be a phase I'm interested in outgrowing. If you haven't gotten there yet, I suspect it may make you feel better about your own timeline.

This book grew out of real life—the joyful, bewildering, middle-of-the-night, please-let-this-be-growth kind of life—alongside years of yoga, inquiry, somatic experiments, and the occasional catastrophic misinterpretation of what I thought the world was trying to tell me. Some pieces arrived with grace. Others arrived by tripping me.

I don't have a neat method or a ten-step plan. I don't even have a three-step plan. What I do have is a working relationship with curiosity, the most reliable force I know for moving me toward feeling more awake and less like I'm rehearsing for a role I never auditioned for. If anything in these pages feels like a companion, something that eases, clarifies, nudges, or just keeps you company, I'm glad. If something doesn't land, you are invited to set it down and keep going.

The word thread appears in the subtitle and throughout the book, so maybe I should say what I mean by it. I don't mean a doctrine, a destiny, or a mystical upgrade. I mean the quiet intelligence you feel before you understand it: the one that shows up as curiosity, sensation, and an inner nudge that says, pay attention here.

Thank you for picking this up. Thank you for reading even a paragraph. The yoke's on us: shared, human, faulty, and, as it turns out, a lot lighter when we stop pretending we're meant to carry it alone.

PROLOGUE

One day, after reading an essay I'd written in my usual style, part earnest inquiry, part caffeinated ramble, my friend Catherine sent an email that stopped me mid-thought. Catherine is a writer, ecologist, and songcrafter with a poet's soul, the rare person who speaks in facts and metaphors at once. Her message was brief, but planetary in impact.

"You probably know that essay means to try."

I did not know that.

But the word fit like a clicked latch. I try not to write to declare. I write to reach, to circle, to test the weight of a question in the hand. Catherine went on: "You try to figure out the world, to figure out love, and then share your explorations."

She suggested these essays might be more than drafts and dispatches. She said that gathered together they might offer a kind of low-lit companionship to anyone who has felt spiritually curious, uncertain, or allergic to certainty itself.

My first thought was: No. Absolutely not. My second thought took its time and refused to leave.

A couple of years later I began excavating. Out came yoga essays, late-night emails, dog-eared notebooks, and reflections written sideways across years I never planned to narrate. None of it was composed with an audience in mind. It was cogitating made visible, the byproduct of someone trying, at times with grace and at others not, to understand the charge between the sacred and the everyday.

A few practical notes before we begin. Some names have been changed for privacy, a few for plausible deniability, and one or two out of a mild and enduring sense of mercy.

I always assumed these scribbles would live and die in digital obscurity, undisturbed except by intermittent hard-drive archaeology. If you're here, reading, you've already outpaced my expectations. Thank you. Truly. It turns out I wasn't writing toward answers at all. I was writing toward company. If any of your questions sound like mine, pull up a chair.

We can wonder at them together.

1

EARLY SKEPTICAL CURIOSITY

I chewed on Jesus in 1966. I'm seven years old, standing in the center aisle of St. Stanislaus in my pristine white dress with lace at the bodice, veil pinned so tight into my scalp it may as well be sacramental. I look like a miniature Polish bride, which is exactly the goal.

Father P, looming like a gothic statue made of cassock and questionable breath, places the sacramental wafer on my tongue. I fold my hands, pivot, and begin the long walk back to our pew. And I chew.

We'd been warned, in no uncertain terms, that letting the host touch your teeth, or worse, chewing it, was flirting with lightning. I chew that wafer like it came from my mother's kitchen and not the body of Christ Himself.

I can feel my parents watching me, so I put on the face I've practiced. Chin lowered, eyes heavy-lidded, a look of solemn reverence that I hoped suggested "This child is terribly holy," even as I masticated the wafer with the enthusiasm of a kid demolishing a vanilla cookie at a church potluck.

I was a devotedly mediocre Catholic. Pious enough to avoid trouble, irreverent enough to survive boredom, and afflicted with what I can only call a fear of being inefficiently sinful. The rules, as I understood them, were these:

- You must confess every sin.
- You must confess weekly.
- You must confess something.
- And you must confess enough to make Father P feel his time was well-spent.

Every week, lined up with the other second graders, I'd go into a mild panic. What had I done wrong? At seven? I hadn't robbed a convenience store. I hadn't murdered anyone. I hadn't coveted my neighbor's wife because I barely understood what coveting was, plus Mrs. W next door had a stiff beehive hairdo that terrified me.

My best friend Sammy and I would huddle in line, whispering in panicked bursts while Sister T glared at us like a hawk choosing which mouse to smite first.

Sammy would twist a lock of her bright red hair so tight around her finger it'd turn purple. She couldn't think unless she was squeezing the life out of that poor strand.

"Tell him you stole a cookie," I whispered.

"I didn't!" she hissed.

"It doesn't matter," I said, already exasperated. "You have to give him something."

She scrunched her freckled nose. "But it's a lie to say I stole a cookie if I didn't."

"Then steal one now," I said, pushing her forward. "Hurry. We don't have all day."

We were seven. We solved existential dilemmas the way seven-year-olds do, inconveniently and with crumbs.

It was during those years that my still-forming brain started having its first questions.

Not gentle questions. Not sweet, cherubic questions. Sharp ones. Uncouth ones. Questions that would have made Sister T clutch her rosary in a death grip.

"If God already knows everything, why do we have to confess?"

"If He made me, why am I in trouble for how He built me?"

"What's the point of guilt if it's baked into the system?"

Nobody wanted to answer these questions. They wanted me to say that "I was sassy to my mother" and accept my three Hail Marys like a good girl. But here's the inconvenient truth about having a curious mind in a fear-based system: You can learn all the rules and still feel like something's off.

By the time I was ten, I had a well-developed internal jury. Twelve hypercritical versions of myself who followed me around, filing charges and objections: You should be better. Why didn't you say that differently? Why didn't you know? Why didn't you do this faster? Why weren't you holy enough to know better?

Fear was my first religion. Curiosity was my first rebellion.

And honestly? Curiosity was the only one that ever felt

like home. Because even then, even as a tiny, trembling girl in an itchy plaid uniform with a cracker melting on her tongue, I could feel it: Somewhere behind the rules and the guilt and the priest's weaponized spittle, something else was moving. Something quieter that didn't demand obedience or perfection or an itemized list of sins.

Something that felt, though I never would've dared say it out loud, like love. But I was reasonably certain that I wasn't wrong.

And that tiny pulse of knowing, barely a tremor, would travel with me through the coming decades of confusion, devotion, rebellion, loss, movement, heartbreak, yoga, Montana, and the slow, steady dissolution of everything I thought I believed.

A thread of curiosity, calling from under the rafters of St. Stan's, from the margins of comic books, from the pages of forbidden Bibles, from the muscle memory of a body trying to tell the truth and, eventually, from the stillness beside my father's deathbed.

But that? That's a story for later.

For now, let me start where it began: with a child, a lace-covered head, a wafer that tasted like paste, and a holy man whose "J"s could baptize the entire front pew.

MAIL-ORDER METAPHYSICS
AND ACCIDENTAL SCRIPTURES

By fourth grade, my metaphysical life had quietly become a side hustle. While the nuns were drilling us on the Baltimore Catechism.

"Who made you?" "God made me." "Why did God make you?" "To know Him, love Him, and serve Him in this world." I could do the whole thing like a trained parrot, yet I was running an entirely separate line of inquiry from my bedroom at home.

The gateway drug?

Comic books.

Not the wholesome ones, necessarily. Not just Archie and Veronica, although I did harbor a deep desire to be a brunette Betty. I gravitated toward the weirder ones: the sci-fi magazines, the ones with aliens that looked suspiciously like shellacked vegetables, the ads for X-ray specs and sea monkeys and "astounding secrets the government doesn't want you to know!"

And tucked between the panels of caped crusaders and

ray guns were the motherlodes: tiny mail-order ads promising enlightenment, psychic powers, hypnotic influence, and—my personal kryptonite—"Guaranteed Contact with Visitors From Other Worlds."

All for $1.25 plus shipping.

I was a child with a modest monthly allowance and an acute urge to understand why the world felt so porous. Like the edges of things weren't entirely sealed. Like if I concentrated hard enough, I could peel back the corner of reality and someone or something might wink back.

So, I mailed cash. Real cash. Crumpled, warm-from-my-hand singles folded into envelopes I stuffed quietly into the mailbox before anyone noticed. Imagine trying that now. A postal worker would probably call a supervisor, a sniffer dog, and three federal agencies.

The materials arrived in plain brown envelopes, as though we were doing something unspeakably illicit. Which, in a good religious small town in 1968, we probably were.

I hid everything under my mattress, right between my diary secured with a flimsy gold lock that could be opened with a strong exhale and my stash of Mad magazines. My bedroom was the perfect covert metaphysical research bunker.

What did I order? Oh, you know, the usual fourth-grade occult starter pack: a booklet on Wicca I did not understand but pretended I did; a pamphlet on self-hypnosis ("Make anyone obey your commands!" Spoiler #1: no); a flimsy "crystal" that turned out to be plastic but still felt powerful in my sweaty little palm; and a pocket-sized, gold-embossed guide promising Three Easy, Guaranteed Steps to Attract a Visit from Space Aliens. Spoiler #2: No aliens showed up.

But I dutifully followed the instructions. The steps were something like:

1. Go to a second-story window around midnight.
2. Close your eyes.
3. Concentrate so hard you can feel your skull vibrate.
4. Wait for friendly extraterrestrials to sense your mental beacon and swoop down to take you on a tour of a distant galaxy.

This struck me as both plausible and preferable to fourth grade. So, there I was, hanging half out of my bedroom window, tiny fingers wrapped around the cold sill, my nightgown puffed around me like I was trying to achieve low-budget flight, whispering into the Wisconsin night:

"Okay... I'm ready. You can come get me now."

Nothing happened. Not even a suspicious rustle in the maple tree.

But I remember that moment with an almost embarrassing fondness. The cold night on my cheeks, the sky like black velvet glittering with Liberace-quality rhinestones, and the delicious anticipation that at any second, I might be swept up and away to a place where everything made more sense.

It was, in retrospect, the first time I ever felt wholly

awake in my body. The first time I realized that a truth can be felt long before it's understood.

∼

Then came the Bible incident. The moment my extracurricular mysticism collided spectacularly with the official storyline.

A comic book ad promised a free leather-bound Bible if you answered their monthly trivia questions. I was already collecting contraband divinity pamphlets. What was one more?

I answered with the earnestness of a child who believed a stamp and an envelope could open the gates of cosmic knowledge.

I even enlisted help.

One question stumped me. Something about the prophet Elijah and a pot of poisoned stew. I didn't know. My best friend Sammy didn't know (she was busy winding her hair around her finger like she was trying to detach it). I asked our classmate who was an altar boy. He shrugged. Finally, I casually slipped the question into conversation with Sister T, trying to sound like I was just curious, not like I needed the key to my future extraterrestrial encounter.

She brightened immediately.

"Oh Anne, what a lovely question! Elijah purified the stew with meal." She said this with the triumphant relief of someone who believed she had just saved a soul from damnation.

My internal jury rolled their eyes in unison.

But I wrote it down anyway. *Meal.* Though honestly, given the context, it sounded like the wrong answer.

A few months later, during our nightly family rosary, the doorbell rang. My mother, eyebrows knit, got up from her knees and went to answer it. I heard muffled voices. Then: "Anne ... ?"

I walked to the front door, kneecaps still red from the carpet.

There they were: two tall Men From Another Religion in stiff black suits with perfectly parted hair and teeth so white they glowed. They looked like someone had ordered missionaries from the Sears catalog.

One held a clipboard. The other held, dear God, my leather Bible.

"We're here to present your daughter with her prize," one said, beaming at my mother.

My mother's face scrolled through a series of micro-expressions: confusion, dawning horror, Midwestern nice, religious discomfort, and then a smile so brittle it could've snapped. I knew I had about four seconds before she asked, "What prize?"

I blurted, "It's for a project! At school! For class! I had to, um, research!"

I grabbed the Bible, thanked the men with the vocal pitch of a terrified soprano, and sprinted back to my room. I shoved my reward under my mattress beside the Wicca pamphlet and under the Mad magazines and whispered to the air, "Please don't let her look under here."

If the aliens were ever going to intervene, that was the moment. But apparently they had *boundaries*.

Later, when the house was quiet again, I slid the Bible out from under the mattress and held it like contraband fireworks. The leather was not, in fact, leather. It was more like a thin layer of pressed cardboard with delusions of grandeur, but it didn't matter. What mattered was this: I had gone looking for something. And the world had responded. Not with celestial beings, yet, but with a book that wasn't sanctioned by the establishment, a book I wasn't supposed to have, a book that felt like a ticket to a wider field of knowing. I didn't read it cover to cover. I was still ten. But I opened it at random, let my finger fall on a sentence, and read:

"Ask, and it shall be given to you."

Well. That felt familiar. I didn't have a name for it yet, but some part of me whispered, See? You're not wrong to be curious. Keep going.

And so I did. Not toward certainty. That ship had sailed. But toward something quieter. Something that hummed beneath the catechism and the comic books and my own private stash of spiritual contraband.

A thread, again. An invitational tug at the heart: Look here. Look again. I didn't know it yet, but the very questions I was sneaking around to ask were beginning to lead me somewhere entirely different. Somewhere I wouldn't find for many years, until a magazine ad for a retreat in Montana landed in my mailbox and everything tilted, just slightly, toward home.

3

FAILING AT BELIEF,
PASSING AT CURIOSITY

At some point in middle school, that volatile chemical mixture of hormones, Aqua Net, and religious dread, I began to realize that my relationship with what everyone called God was lopsided.

Not broken. Not hostile. Just tilted, like a picture frame that refuses to stay straight no matter how many times you nudge it.

On Sundays, I'd file into Mass with my family, dip my fingers into the holy water, kneel, genuflect (right knee, always), and try to arrange my features into the correct balance of humility and alertness. Too solemn and Mom and Dad worried. Too relaxed and Sister T deployed her laser-pointer eyes.

But inside? Inside I felt like a friendly trespasser. A well-meaning tourist in a foreign country where everyone else seemed fluent. They all knew when to bow, when to stand, when to recite the Profession of Faith without checking the missalette. They believed with the kind of certainty I could only fake: a glossy, luminous certainty that I envied the way a girl with thin, slippery hair envies someone with an effortless thick braid.

Meanwhile, I carried my private cargo of questions like contraband up the nave:

- *If God is love, why is He so mad all the time?*
- *If Jesus died for our sins, do we get a receipt?*
- *If God made me, didn't He also make the part of me that asks these questions?*
- *And if so, why do adults look at me like I'm trying to ruin Christmas every time I ask one?*

This was not the kind of critical inquiry our parish encouraged. No one said it outright, of course. But you could feel it. A gentle, pervasive *don't poke the holy bear*. So, I did what any shy girl with a subversive streak would do: I stopped asking out loud and started asking inward. Not praying, at least not in the way I'd been taught. More like ... listening.

Leaning in. Checking the edges. And every time I turned inward, I kept bumping into something or someone that felt nothing like a God of *rules* and everything like a God of *yes*.

A spaciousness. A quiet. A presence that didn't seem bothered by my doubts at all. If anything, it seemed amused.

This was the era when I started realizing that adults, while often kind, were not necessarily reliable narrators. They contradicted themselves. They said one thing in the parish hall and another in the car. They preached forgiveness while holding grudges for decades. They said, "God will smite you for lying," then fibbed to each other with a smile so tight you could've snapped it like a communion wafer.

I don't mean this unkindly. I loved them. But I also saw through them. And once you see a thing, you can't unsee it, no matter how hard you try.

So, I created my own quiet church composed of:

- a bedroom window cracked open to the night;
- a stack of forbidden pamphlets;
- a plastic "crystal" that I treated like a sacred relic;
- and the sense, growing, humming, that truth wasn't handed down from on high so much as felt from within.

If the Church wanted me to memorize answers, this other thing, whatever it was, wanted me to notice. To wonder. To stay awake.

Curiosity was sanctuary and loophole. Rebellion with training wheels. It didn't demand perfection or threaten lightning bolts. It didn't care if I believed the right things in the right order with the right posture at the right time.

Curiosity just kept whispering: Pay attention. There's something here worth noticing. You don't have to know. Just look. I didn't tell anyone this. How could I? I barely had language for it myself.

And then adolescence arrived. Loud, dramatic, and

entirely uninterested in my metaphysical musings. Years of detours and derailments and survivals began stacking themselves like unsorted mail. (We'll get there when we get there; for now, we keep the camera panned back.)

But even in the messiest middle, that early shimmer stayed with me. Not as a belief, but as a compass. A quiet north. A thing that whispered: There's more. You don't have to swallow the story whole. You can keep following the questions.

And eventually, those questions would lead me to a different kind of practice, a different kind of prayer, a different kind of teacher. One who would never dream of telling me to stop asking questions. But that's still a chapter away.

Following the Thread. *At this point in my life, I still thought curiosity was a personality trait. Something I possessed, or maybe something I couldn't help. I didn't yet recognize it as a skill or a practice or a form of intelligence that could be cultivated.*

I believed I was failing at belief, when what I was doing was learning how to listen without a script. I hadn't found yoga yet. I didn't have language for embodiment, nervous systems, or inner authority. All I knew was that whenever I tried to force certainty, something in me went quiet, and whenever I stopped trying to know, something else leaned forward.

Looking back, I can see that I wasn't wandering aimlessly. I was circling and testing and learning the difference between

*answers that landed in my head and those that settled some-
where deeper, with weight and warmth. I didn't know it then,
but this was already training. Not toward a system or a teacher,
but toward a way of trusting what registers before it explains
itself. The thread was already in my hand. I just hadn't learned
how to feel it yet.*

4

THE LUCKIEST START

If my early years gave me anything. it was a low-grade allergy to people who claimed absolute authority. I didn't know that at the time. I assumed I was "sensitive" or constitutionally incapable of blindly following instructions. It never occurred to me that this wiring might, much later, spare me from some of yoga's more theatrical corners.

My resistance to being bossed around didn't appear out of thin air. My mother, whom I adored, also had a charming aversion to instructions, especially the printed kind. If something came with assembly guidelines, she'd push them aside with the confidence of a woman who believed furniture should bend to her will, not the other way around. "I don't need anyone telling me what to do," she'd mutter, and I'd watch her fearlessly, if not always successfully, reinvent the intended purpose of assorted screws and dowels. I didn't recognize it then, but the part of me that bristled at rigid authority may have been inherited.

But before I ever encountered any of that, I stumbled, quite accidentally, into the softest possible beginning.

It started with Enid, my first real yoga teacher. A steady, quietly radiant woman who could have been cast as "kind neighbor with excellent banana bread" in a feel-good movie. She didn't sweep into class with mystique or charisma. She didn't posture or pontificate. She didn't preach. She certainly didn't demand.

She simply shared yoga. And that was revolutionary.

There was a gentleness to her presence, a kind of human permission slip. In Enid's class, nobody flinched if you wobbled. Nobody furrowed their brow at your toes. Nobody patrolled your breathing patterns or corrected you like you were a spiritual misdemeanor waiting to happen.

It was the first environment of my adult life in which I wasn't bracing.

Do you know that feeling when a space feels so safe that even your shoulders, those overachievers, finally go off duty? Mine had been on a decades-long shift with no union break.

I didn't realize yoga was slipping under my skin the way water soaks into a parched plant: quietly, steadily, without asking permission. My shoulders started dropping of their own accord. My thoughts stopped pacing like caged animals. My nervous system, trained for decades to anticipate criticism, began to unclench.

I didn't "fall in love with yoga." That phrase is too dramatic, too Hollywood. It was more like discovering a warm room you keep wanting to return to without understanding why.

And then one ordinary Sunday morning, everything tilted slightly.

I remember driving home after one of Enid's classes, an unremarkable Sunday, the kind where the world feels half-awake and the air is still deciding if it wants to be warm. Nothing dramatic had happened in class. No spiritual fireworks. No visions or mysterious tingling at the base of my spine. Just movement, breath, and the kind of quiet that sneaks up on you.

But somewhere between a long forward fold and a surprisingly sweet *savasana*, something subtle clicked. I didn't know what it was. I still don't. Driving home, I felt an effervescent bubbling. An internal lift. A soft shimmer of recognition. It was as if I had latched onto a golden thread, one I hadn't known existed until that moment, and it hummed with the unmistakable sense of rightness.

Not perfection or escape. Not "I've found my calling." Just: "Oh. There you are. I didn't even know you were missing."

I had this soothing, welcome whisper of knowing that whatever unfolded in the rest of my life—losses, surprises, inevitable unravellings—something in me now had an anchor. A soft companion strong enough to see me through. I whispered "Thank you" into my empty car, like a person who had momentarily forgotten that dashboards don't require gratitude. It was absurd and real. And it stayed.

Have you ever had a moment like that, an ordinary

instant that somehow rearranged something inside you? Not dramatic, not cinematic, just undeniably, quietly true? Sometimes the smallest moments mark us the longest.

I didn't know then how rare this start was. I didn't know many people entered yoga through intensity or acrobatics or the gravitational pull of a charismatic teacher with a cult-sized following. I just knew that I'd found something quietly medicinal. And looking back, I realize how fortunate that was. The yoga world, beautiful as it can be, is also littered with fallen idols, broken trusts, and teachers whose "awakening" turned out to be marketing strategy. I've had friends who were hurt, disillusioned, left picking up pieces they never expected to drop. Somehow, none of that ever touched me. I slipped through the whole thing like someone wandering through a minefield with beginner's luck and alert guardian spirits.

And that gentle, organic, unforced opening was the soil that later allowed me to receive the teaching that would inform my entire path: what Erich Schiffmann calls Freedom Yoga. The yoga of feeling inward, of learning to detect and trust your inner signals and what he calls divine guidance. The yoga of a teacher saying, in essence, "I can't decide your life for you, but I can help you get quiet enough, long enough, to hear the part of you that can."

At that time, I hadn't yet met Erich. I hadn't been to Montana. I hadn't walked into the big lodge at the Feathered Pipe Ranch with the elk head and the morning light slanting onto the big log walls like a blessing. I hadn't felt the way a true teacher can redirect your life by handing your inner authority back to you.

But the blueprint was already being laid. Enid gave me room to breathe, space to feel, permission to go slow. My body began thawing from the inside out. And she gave me something else I didn't see clearly until much later: she made me available to receive deeper teachings without getting tangled in hierarchy or doctrine. She softened me enough to trust resonance, not rules.

She didn't turn me into a yogi but she turned me into someone who could listen and feel. And that, as it turns out, was everything. The joy I felt in those early days wasn't flashy, but a joy of stumbling into a path I didn't know I needed and realizing, long before I could explain it, that it would walk with me through the rest of my days.

And if you think back on your own life, just briefly and gently, have there been moments like that? Quiet beginnings that didn't announce themselves but, looking back, changed the whole trajectory? Sometimes life shifts with a whisper instead of a thunderclap.

5

FREEDOM AND
FEATHERED PIPEDREAMS

I found yoga because I thought I was trying to repair myself. I stayed because a teacher who looked like he might have been dropped out of the sky by a benevolent cosmic prankster kept insisting, with impossible gentleness, that I wasn't broken. His name was (and still is) Erich Schiffmann, though if you'd asked me back then, I might've described him as "a tall, gentle, California creature who teaches yoga like he's receiving radio signals from another dimension."

I first encountered him the way important teachers always seem to enter my life: by accident, or fate, or whatever name you give to the background choreography that happens when you're not paying attention. I was flipping through an issue of *Yoga Journal* back when it was equal parts spiritual musings, "how to deepen your practice," and organic tampon ads, when I saw it: a weeklong retreat in Montana with a teacher I'd only seen in a dreamy video filmed in the desert with Ali MacGraw.

A whole week in a place I'd never heard of. Led by a man who looked like he'd stepped directly out of a dream sequence. It felt a bit reckless and delicious. Without thinking too hard, since that's the fastest way to kill magic, I signed up. I told myself I'd go once. Just one weeklong summer yoga fling with myself. Of course, that one time turned into a week every summer until he retired from the Ranch. Some loves are quiet but magnetic like that.

The first time I saw him in person, he was walking down the gravel path from the main lodge. Very tall, long curls catching the light, sparkling eyes that looked both innocent and wildly attuned, and the kindest, most welcoming smile.

He wore a green shirt, soft pants, and, as though the universe wanted to add a punchline, bright orange Crocs. He radiated a kind of cosmic-teddy-bear luminosity. Nothing about him said "follow me," "obey me," or "I have the answers."

Everything about him said, "You are already whole. Let's see if you can feel it." For someone raised in a world where authority was a top-down enterprise and confidence was often confused with correctness, his humility was disarming. Revolutionary, even.

People used to ask him, "So... what style of yoga do you teach?" He'd tilt his head, owl-like, curious, and say, "Welp, I guess we call it Freedom Yoga." Which is hilarious, because Freedom Yoga appears on exactly zero official lists of yoga styles.

He trained with B.K.S. Iyengar himself and was on the brink of certification—capital letters, official recognition, the whole canon—when a senior teacher informed him, "You're not really teaching Iyengar Yoga anymore. You're teaching something else. Something like cocktail yoga." Cocktail yoga. As in, "Lovely, darling, but concerning."

And so he didn't become an Iyengar teacher. He became fully Erich. Or maybe he just stopped pretending to be anything else. His teaching wasn't about rebelling against structure; it was about encouraging us to listen for inner structure. To prioritize felt experience over performance. To trust the intelligence that hums inside the body.

He saved me from the almost universal yoga trap: believing the teacher knows more about your body and heart than you do.

A few years into attending his retreats, I found myself walking the winding path toward the main lodge on a crisp morning when something quietly life-changing happened. We fell into step together. I told him how incredible the morning class had been, how moved everyone was, how grateful. He stopped walking, turned toward me, and said with absolute sincerity, "Oh good, because I was nervous."

Nervous. Erich. Nervous. I nearly tripped. This man, this gentle giant whose presence felt like being hugged by the universe, still got nervous before teaching. He wasn't telegraphing certainty or building a persona. He was human. Listening inward. Doing his best. Trusting whatever whispered back. And in that moment, I thought: Oh. If he can be nervous and still show up, maybe I don't have to be perfect either. It was a small liberation, but a seismic one.

Years later, long after he stepped back from teaching at

the Ranch, I realized how lucky I'd been in the yoga world. Somehow, without strategy or savvy, I landed with teachers who weren't secretly tyrants, narcissists, or future documentary subjects. I watched friends and fellow practitioners survive devastating falls from grace in the yoga world. Scandals. Manipulation. Big betrayals. Whole communities imploding. Meanwhile, my biggest hardship was learning what to do with my arms in Warrior II and questioning life choices during long holds in pigeon pose.

At some point during those early years—I can't remember if it was on a walk, over breakfast, or during one of our rambling conversations by the lake—Erich told me he always recited something to himself before teaching. Not a pep talk or a visualization, but a passage from *A Course in Miracles* called the "Special Principles of Miracle Workers." He didn't share it dramatically. Just quietly, like something that had become woven into him. The lines stayed with me:

I am here only to be truly helpful.

I do not have to worry about what to say or do, because He Who sent me will direct me.

I am content to be wherever I am, knowing He goes there with me.

I will be healed as I let Him teach me to heal.

Over time, I understood "the principles" not as reaching for something outside myself but as opening to the larger capital-s Self. That spacious, quiet awareness that feels older than my biography. The one that surfaces when I stop driving my life like it's an uphill manual transmission.

Before I share yoga with a class now, I breathe and let those lines rise. "I am here only to be truly helpful." It's a bow of trust toward whatever-it-is that's wiser than my personality. It feels like surrendering to an inner guidance system, one that only comes online when I stop insisting that I'm supposed to have all the answers.

This was a big beginning. Not fireworks or feats of strength. A teacher who taught me how to listen to myself.

6

———————

THE PLACE THAT REARRANGED ME

I didn't know the first time I went to Montana that a place could quietly rearrange the furniture in your inner world without asking permission. I'd come for a yoga retreat; I left with the sense that some places aren't retreats at all. They're soft interventions, delivered, in the case of the Feathered Pipe Ranch, by aspens, mountain air, and a very tall man wearing Crocs.

The first time I went, I stayed in a tipi. Not to be confused with glamping. A real one: lodgepole pine poles wrapped in canvas, a cot, and an opening at the top that paid no attention to comfort. In theory, that opening could be adjusted; opened to invite light and air, closed against rain and cold. In practice, it required a long pole, a precise hook-and-lift maneuver, and a level of coordination I did not possess.

The idea was to stand outside the tipi, insert the pole into a small fold near the top, lift, and then walk it carefully around the circumference to set it just right, stepping over rocks, navigating branches, maintaining balance. What happened in real life was that I tripped, lurched, and circled in wide, uncertain arcs, like a long-limbed animal not yet fluent in gravity. The whole thing unfolded with the seriousness of a silent-film scene: sincere effort, incorrect execution. I eventually retreated inside, suitcase at my feet, wondering if this was a good idea.

That night, lying rigid on the cot, I heard snorting just outside the canvas. My mind went straight to bears. Do bears snort, I wondered, holding my breath like it might help. In the morning, I learned it had been a mule deer. Apparently bears have better manners.

Another night, an epic hailstorm slammed the valley. Ice and rain pelted the canvas so hard it felt inches from my face. The walls soaked through. I lay there half-awake, clutching my camera to my chest like a life raft, trying to keep it dry while the storm did whatever it pleased.

And still, despite all of that, I felt better deep down into my cells in that canvas dwelling than I had in years. There was something about breathing cold, clean air all night. About waking before dawn and looking straight up through the opening at the top of the tipi to a sky freckled with stars, bigger and brighter than the ones I'd stared at as a child leaning out my bedroom window in Wisconsin, quietly pleading with aliens to take me somewhere else.

The magic wasn't flashy and it didn't announce itself, but it seeped, into my bones, into my breath, into the part of me that had always known that being a little exposed might be the point.

Each morning, I walked from my tipi to the lodge along a gently curving path, pine needles and twigs soft underfoot. I could feel the reflexes I'd carried for decades still humming, shoulders slightly lifted, jaw subtly set, attention scanning for cues. The mountains didn't seem to notice. The air felt wider than I was used to, as if it had fewer opinions. The silence had weight. It didn't rush to fill itself. With each step downhill, something in me seemed to lag behind like some internal supervisor clocking out early.

Just as the trees aligned themselves into a cathedral of light, I'd hear it behind me: whff-whff-whff. Gravel. Rubber. The unmistakable sound of Erich's Crocs.

I laughed out loud.

That sound—ridiculous, grounding—snapped me back into my body. It felt like a reminder from the universe: yes, presence and mystery, but also Crocs. Don't get carried away.

Mornings unfolded slowly. Mist lifted off the lake in visible breaths. Deer stood at the edge of the treeline, watchful and unimpressed. I'd sit on the dock after practice, legs dangling, noticing for the first time in my life how little instruction the water required to be itself.

One morning, during class, Erich spoke in that unhurried way he had when something mattered. He said, almost conversationally, "Death is a fake." Someone chuckled. Someone else shifted. He went on with something I remember as: "The thing you discover after you die is that you didn't."

If you hear that in yoga, it's reasonable to wonder

whether someone has been overly generous with the incense. But when he said it, something in me went still. Not fear. Recognition. Like a tuning fork struck somewhere behind my sternum. I didn't understand it, not intellectually, but my body sure did. A quiet internal click, as if something old had just been named.

Days passed. Nothing dramatic happened. And yet, day by day, something in me softened. Not because I was trying to be open, but because I stopped bracing. My shoulders dropped when they weren't being watched. My breath lengthened without instruction. It felt like the way your body loosens when it finally believes no one in the room is waiting to critique you.

Then the tears arrived.

Not once or twice, but in bewildering waves. Sitting by the lake. Walking through the meadow. Lying in *savasana* beneath the elk head in the lodge, a benevolent witness to so many unravelings. I'd be overtaken by sobbing that didn't feel sad exactly, more like relief. As if something deep in my system had been holding on for a very long time and had finally been told it could let go.

One afternoon stands out. Class had ended. Warm light slanted through the lodge windows. The scent of ponderosa drifted in. I walked down the gravel path toward the lake, body soft, mind unusually quiet. Halfway there, something opened. Not fireworks. Just a steady swell in my chest. A gentle certainty.

At that exact moment, a raven swooped down and dropped a pinecone at my feet with impeccable timing. I stopped, laughed, and bent to pick it up.

Message received.

I didn't know then how comforting and familiar that feeling was. During World War II, my father taught himself to play the concertina. He also taught himself to bake, a skill that would become his vocation once the war ended. I've always loved that these two things arrived together: bread and music. Sustenance and solace. Both made by hand.

Music stayed with him for the rest of his life. It was where he went to feel good, and where he took others when they needed it too. He loved nothing more than playing for people. Family, friends, anyone within earshot. In his mid-eighties, he used to head off to the senior center to play polka music "for the old folks," which never failed to delight him, since by any reasonable measure, he was one of them.

One of his music-making buddies built makeshift percussion instruments out of spare parts and mischief. For my dad, he made something called a rhythm stick. It was a four-and-a-half-foot-long pole, about chest-high, with a rubber cap on the bottom. Pie tins were held in place with two large, tight springs and filled with little noise-making beans. A big bell was mounted near the top. The idea was percussive accompaniment. You lifted the stick and pounded it on the downbeat. Then you used a drumstick to thwap the springs so they rattled against the pie tins. And at key moments—this was important—you hit the bell for emphasis.

As a kid, I was always a little embarrassed to play with him. Polka music was not doing me any social favors. Still, he insisted I had "the best sense of rhythm," which I did (objectively and undisputedly) and he loved having someone join him. So there we'd be: him squeezing the concertina, me bang-thwap-thwap (ding!), trying very hard not to be seen by anyone I knew.

The grin on his face made it impossible not to smile. It was wide, boyish, utterly unselfconscious. Music, for him, wasn't performance or polish. It was a shared pulse and a way to make a room lighter. A way to say, without saying much at all, we're alive, and this is fun.

By the end of the week at the Ranch, I wasn't leaving with a philosophy. I wasn't carrying answers. What I had was something quieter and more durable: the sense of a thread in my hand, a companioning yes that whispered, Stay close. Keep listening. Have some fun.

When Erich eventually stepped back from teaching at the Ranch, my relationship with the place didn't step back with him. The land itself seemed to take over. I kept returning. The Ranch shifted from "where Erich teaches" to "where my life keeps unfolding." It threaded itself into my teaching, my listening, my understanding of what it means to trust what I feel rather than what I'm told.

I didn't yet know how essential that thread would become, or how it would meet me in grief, or at my father's bedside, or in the quiet moments when certainty fails. But even then, early on, I knew this much: I had come to the Feathered Pipe Ranch once. And I would come back.

Some places hold your life and teach you, wordlessly, how to arrive inside it.

7

LEARNING TO TEACH WITHOUT PRETENDING TO KNOW EVERYTHING

When I look back at my early days of teaching yoga, I'm struck by how unaware I was of how unprepared I felt. That is, until the moment other human beings started doing what I said.

My "final practice class" at the end of my first teacher training is seared into my nervous system. The room held twenty-some kind, trusting souls sitting on their mats, waiting. I stood at the front, heart already racing, trying to project an air of knowing while absolutely, unequivocally not knowing.

I offered my first instruction. "Lift your arms overhead."

And then, to my horror, everyone did it.

No hesitation. No skepticism. Forty arms shot skyward in obedient unison. Inside my head I was shrieking, Oh no, please don't do that just because I said it. I barely trust myself. Why are you trusting me? Outwardly, of course, I smiled serenely, as if this were all unfolding according to plan.

That moment rewired me, not because of the responsibility, though that landed too, but because I saw how much authority is projected onto whoever happens to be sitting in the teacher's seat. Even if that person is internally negotiating panic and trying to remember which side moves first in a twist.

Then came the moment that nearly sent me running out of the building. We were in table pose. Hands and knees. Four points of contact. Arguably one of the most stable shapes in all of yoga. A pose so structurally secure that drunken toddlers and golden retrievers can manage it without instruction.

I offered a simple cue.

"Gently shift your weight a little forward and back."

And then I heard it. A tiny, startled yelp. A collapse. A thud. I looked over just in time to see the woman on the mat beside me fall out of table pose.

Fall.

Out of table pose.

She clutched her hip and whispered, mortified, "My hip."

Time slowed. My body froze. My already beating-too-fast heart slammed harder. I crouched beside her, asking if she was okay, nodding as she said yes, trying to sound calm while a familiar inner chant surged. I can't do anything right. I suck. I should not be here.

This was my test class. An assigned observer sat in the room, a good friend and a teacher I deeply admired. All the old reflexes arrived at once. Perfectionism. Shame. The certainty that one mistake had revealed the whole truth about me.

The woman was fine. Her hip was fine. Her pride took a small hit. Mine took a larger one.

Something else cracked open. That moment taught me something I hadn't wanted to know. Even the gentlest cue can be misheard. Even the safest shape can unravel. People don't receive instructions in a vacuum. They receive them through their history, their fear, their eagerness to get it right.

It would take me years, decades honestly, to live inside that truth without becoming either controlling or paralyzed. To navigate the space between Simon Says and a deeper invitation. Helping people sense alignment, safety, and authenticity from the inside.

Around that same time, quieter questions began tapping at the edges of my training.

I would cue poses the way I'd been taught, saying the words out loud while thinking, I don't know why we do it this way. I'd been trained to "teach from the chakras," to divide the body into zones and themes, and I want to say clearly that this approach has helped many people. I was just not one of them. For me, it felt like slicing a living organism into parts. My body didn't experience itself that way. It felt whole, continuous, responsive. One conversation, not many compartments.

Those doubts weren't dramatic, but they were persistent. The tip of an iceberg.

Erich used to say, "If you want to be in alignment, let

yourself be aligned." He didn't mean stacking joints like a diagram. He meant listening. Feeling. Paying attention to what arises.

(Erich is so cool.)

His humility had already imprinted itself on me. It lived somewhere in the back of my mind like a steady suggestion. Don't be the authority. Be the invitation.

So my teaching got awkward.

I started saying things like, "Here's an idea. See if it feels right for you." Or, "You might try this, or not." Or, "Ignore me completely if your body disagrees." It was a blend of enthusiasm, apology, and hope. Messy. Experimental. Occasionally incoherent.

And curiously, people seemed to like it.

They softened and sometimes laughed. They lightened up and stopped trying so hard to look like they were doing yoga correctly. Classes became less about following instructions and more about shared attention. I watched students make small, brave choices. Adjusting a pose without asking. Resting without permission. Trusting sensation over performance.

Slowly, I understood that teaching wasn't about transmitting knowledge. It was about midwifing curiosity. About helping people stop outsourcing their wisdom, not just to me, but to the entire culture of correctness we swim in.

Later, when grief arrived, the kind that rearranges the furniture of a life, my teaching deepened in a way no certification ever could. Presence stopped being a concept and became a necessity. Listening stopped being performative and became survival.

Teaching is where I learned to follow the thread. Loss is where I learned why. But that's the next chapter. The one where everything I'd been practicing, from childhood intuition to orange Crocs to Montana's quiet insistence, finally coalesced into something unmistakably true. I didn't yet know how literal that learning would become.

8

THE SPACE BETWEEN MINUTES

I didn't know life was about to break open that January day. What I did know was that my dad, my gentle, steady, ninety-two-year-old dad, was suddenly "not doing at all well," according to my mother, who had a lifelong habit of protecting me from panic by offering the least alarming version of the truth.

Then came the call where her voice changed. The one where "not doing well" quietly turned into "you should probably come home."

What followed was a frantic scan of flight options. There weren't many. Nothing lined up in a way that made sense for a my-father-is-dying-and-I-need-to-get-there-now emergency. The best I could manage landed me in an airport seventy miles from the hospital. Seventy miles is not far unless your father's heart is failing fast. Then it's an eternity.

When the plane touched down in Milwaukee for the layover, I walked off feeling like my bones had been hollowed out and filled with electricity. I paced the carpeted terminal, half-praying, half-bargaining, trying to remember how breathing worked. Overhead, the news was doing what the news does, narrating some other catastrophe in bright colors. The chyron announced that Illinois Governor Rod Blagojevich had been convicted of corruption the day before. It felt like watching a play in a language I no longer spoke.

Somewhere in that haze, I called my friend Judy.

Judy, rest her soul, was equal parts mystic and drill sergeant. I told her I was terrified. That I couldn't bear the thought of losing my dad. That I didn't know how to manage what was coming.

She did not soothe me.

Instead, in a voice that could have cut steel, she said, "DROP FEAR. NOW."

I went quiet. She softened her tone, but not her message.

"You are about to walk into one of the most important moments of your life," she said. "Don't let fear be the thing that runs it. If you let terror take over, you'll miss what's unfolding and what's real. And he will feel that. Be with him and the experience, not your fear."

I stood there, phone pressed to my ear, feet rooted to the airport carpet as people rolled suitcases around me.

She kept going. "You don't want your father's last experience of you to be your panic. You want to meet him. Really meet him. This is sacred terrain. Don't let fear steal it."

She wasn't telling me not to cry. She wasn't telling me

to be strong. She was asking me to choose something deeper than terror.

I didn't have any better ideas, so I listened.

When I boarded the small plane to Appleton, I started talking to Dad in my mind. I'm coming. I'm on my way. I love you. Somehow everything is okay. I don't know how, but it is.

Somewhere over the icy Wisconsin skies, something shifted. I felt us link up, as if a filament stretched between his awareness and mine. My fear didn't disappear, but it loosened. In its place came a steady sense that we were already in conversation.

For a moment, everything stilled. Then the practical world surged back in.

The drive from the airport to the hospital felt suspended, like driving through a photograph. The January sky was Windex blue, winter sunlight bouncing brutally off the snow. The roads were mostly clear. I heard a quiet inner nudge. Don't speed. Don't panic. Pay attention. Just get there. I drove only a little over the speed limit. Hands at ten and two. Heart racing, body obedient.

At the hospital entrance, the heavy doors sighed open into that peculiar mix of antiseptic and fluorescent-lit normalcy. I went straight to the reception desk. The woman working there recognized me instantly. She was a longtime neighbor of my parents.

"Anne! Oh my gosh, how are you? What's new?"

She knew Dad was hospitalized, not that he was dying. I tried to answer politely, but every second of small talk felt like someone dimming the lights on time I could never get back. Inside, some wild animal part of me was howling, I need his room number. Now.

I cut her off as kindly as I could and made my way to him. I can still feel the hallway under my shoes as I walked toward his door through a long tunnel of tile and air and dread.

When I stepped into the room, everything tightened and expanded at once. My family was gathered. My mother stood at his bedside, grief forming a halo around her. Machines hummed and blinked. The monitor traced thin lines. My unconscious father lay there, oddly small for a man whose presence had filled entire rooms.

When I came into the room, I remember a small stir of attention. Someone noticed the monitor register a brief change, a flicker of activity. "He knows you're here," someone said.

I dropped my bags and went to him. Slipped my hand under the blanket to find his. It wasn't very warm. My brother murmured, "His hands are getting colder."

Judy's earlier command roared back through my body. DROP FEAR. NOW.

I don't know how to explain what happened next in a way that satisfies the rational mind. Rationality was not running the show. Something in me shifted. I let go, not of him, but of the story that I was losing him. I leaned in, rested my head near his shoulder, whispered some love, and something between us merged.

The best I can say is that my awareness stepped through a doorway and found his. There was no terror there. No narrative. No bargaining. Only presence. Only Dad.

When the monitor line went flat a couple of short minutes later, nothing in that presence changed. A nurse came in not long after. She must have been monitoring things from the station. In a voice that sounded almost casual, the same one you'd use to say it was time to refill the water pitcher, she said, "Ohhh, looks like somebody went and expired, huh?"

Not unkindly. Efficiently.

The room erupted in sobs and stunned silence, as it should have. But the strangest thing was that I felt all of him more clearly than I ever had when he was alive in his body. If anything, he felt more expansive.

I heard myself say quietly, unable to pretend, "You guys, he's okay. He's more than okay."

Later, when the shock softened enough for practical thoughts, I tried to make sense of the timing. The math didn't compute.

The trek from the airport to the hospital should have taken at least eighty or ninety minutes. That doesn't include landing, the rental car, scraping the windshield, the parking garage, the walk to his room.

But the time of death was forty-five minutes after my plane landed. By any calculation, I should have arrived after he died. I don't claim to know what happened. I'm not suggesting anything supernatural. I'm saying only that what clocks measure and what presence knows aren't always aligned. At his bedside, whatever the clock insisted, I was exactly where I needed to be.

After a brief flurry of hospital tasks, I followed Mom home. She had been married to my father for nearly sixty years, had just watched him take his last breath, and within half an hour she was sending me to the grocery store.

"People will be coming by," she said. "We need something for them to eat."

I found myself pushing a cart down fluorescent aisles, feeling like I was walking underwater. I was still with Dad in that strange, luminous way. And yet I was also selecting crackers. Staring at sale tags. Watching strangers debate salsa.

My father had just died. And there were two-for-one potato chips.

In the days and weeks that followed, grief behaved less like a sequence of stages and more like weather. I cried in expected places and bizarre ones. I felt shredded and grateful, broken and expanded. I moved through logistics with Mom and my siblings and laughed hard enough at times that I was sure Dad was in on the joke.

Underneath it all was something new. A quiet, unshakable knowing that the thread I'd felt since childhood had just revealed itself in the most intimate way possible.

I didn't lose my father that day. What I lost was the sense that love ends where bodies do, or that it keeps time.

ollowing the Thread. Up until then, the thread *could still be dismissed. A temperament. A habit of paying attention. Something I was probably over-interpreting. My father's death took that option away.*

I didn't show up calm or prepared or spiritually fluent. I showed up late, shaking, my coat still on, my bag dropped where it fell. I took his hand without knowing what I was supposed to say and found myself listening instead.

This wasn't belief or courage. It wasn't trust, exactly either. It was closer to muscle memory, like knowing how to balance when the ground shifts under your feet. I didn't rise to the occasion. I was steadied by it.

What surprised me wasn't the intensity, but how ordinary it felt in my body. The room. The machines. The weight of his hand. Breath happening. Then not. Afterward, I couldn't talk myself out of what had happened. Whatever I'd been doing all those years such as standing at windows, paying attention in quiet rooms, noticing when something softened or tightened, it had all held.

Nothing about it made things easier but it did make them unmistakable. And once that line was crossed, there was no crossing back. I could still doubt, question, and get lost. But I could no longer pretend I didn't know where to stand when everything else fell away.

9

———

UNLEARNING

If yoga has a secret curriculum, the part you only discover after the honeymoon stage, it's this: unlearning is the real practice. The poses are decoys. Very bendy, photogenic decoys.

I didn't understand that for a long time. Partly because I was a dutiful student, trained from childhood to plan, perform, and perfect. And partly because the yoga world, like every other human ecosystem, comes with unspoken rules. Some are useful. Some are absurd. All eventually require scrutiny and, if you're lucky, a slow dismantling.

One of the first things I had to unlearn was the quiet belief that poses said something about a person. Not aesthetically. Morally. Spiritually. Somewhere along the way, certain shapes had become symbols. A deep back-bend meant openness. A solid handstand meant courage. A serene lotus suggested enlightenment, or at least that you had your life together.

It wasn't just the moral symbolism. We also trafficked

in a whole folklore of physiological promises. Forward folds were "soothing." Backbends were "energizing." Twists, somehow, were detoxifying, as if your liver took coffee breaks and needed spinal wringing to get back to work. These ideas were repeated so often they acquired the status of fact, passed teacher to teacher like well-meaning hearsay. Early on, I taught some of them myself. Not because I had evidence, but because they sounded yogic and everyone else seemed to be saying them with impressive confidence.

None of this made yoga bad or useless. But it revealed something important: we are very good at mistaking repetition for truth. And very bad at pausing to ask whether our actual experience matches the story.

Underneath both the symbolism and the folklore was the same habit of mind. We had turned shapes into meaning. These were postural idols. Beautiful, interesting, sometimes helpful shapes, yes. Still just shapes. Temporary arrangements of bone, muscle, and breath. They might reveal biomechanics or habitual tension, but they couldn't reliably tell you anything about someone's worth, insight, or inner life. If they could, yoga teachers would be far easier to spot in the wild.

That realization softened something in me. It loosened the subtle hierarchy of "advanced" and "beginner," not in terms of skill, but imagined spiritual significance. It made room for something truer: practice isn't measured in shapes. It's measured in sincerity, which inconveniently refuses to be photographed.

Like most teachers, I learned this the hard way. When I

first started teaching, I thought my job was to keep people perfectly safe. No risks. No surprises. No deviations from the curriculum. If I didn't anticipate every wobble, every misunderstanding, every possible misstep, someone would topple over. Or worse, judge me, possibly while holding a yoga strap.

So I over-prepared. I over-explained. I over-efforted. My early classes were so heavily narrated it's a miracle anyone could hear themselves think. I talked people in and out of poses like I was defusing a bomb. Left foot here. Soften this. Now soften the inner edges of your inner edges. That's the sort of sentence that happens when you're trying very hard to sound like a yoga teacher.

Meanwhile, my inner monologue was in full panic. Why are you all just doing what I say? This feels like far too much authority for someone who still occasionally forgets which side is left. Or where she put her glasses. Or why she walked into the kitchen.

Then there was the day something began to crack open.

I was standing at the front of the room, glancing at my carefully crafted class plan. The sequence followed all the accepted rules. Logical progression. Smart build. Nothing risky. Nothing controversial. Almost certainly approved by the invisible powers that be, whoever they were that week.

As I demonstrated the next pose, I noticed something uncomfortable. When I practiced on my own, my body almost never did it this way. It always asked for a small detour. A different transition. An elongated pause that made no sense on paper but felt inevitable in real time. Nothing dramatic. Just a quiet, persistent request.

And there it was. The familiar tightening. The moment where you can either override your own experience or listen.

I remember thinking, What if I cue this the way my body actually does it? What if I set the rules aside and no one reports me? My heart picked up, because this was not what I had been trained to do. Training rewarded clarity, authority, and clean lines. This felt a good deal messier.

I paused. The room got quiet in that way it does when no one knows what's coming next. Then I offered the cue differently. Not as a correction, but as an invitation. I told them what I felt in my own body and suggested they see what theirs had to say.

No one revolted. No one stormed out. The ceiling didn't cave in. What did happen was subtler and far more interesting. The room softened. Breath changed. People lingered inside the shape instead of rushing through it. And for the first time, I felt less like I was leading a class and more like I was listening alongside them.

It became harder over time to follow sequences that didn't feel true in my own body. More important, I started to crack the challenging code of how to share inner listening itself and appreciating the few teachers I'd known who managed to do just that. Not by abandoning alignment or throwing away useful cues, but by sharing ideas on how to sense, test, and respond. How to take a brief detour and notice what happens. How to build trust not in me, but in their own experience.

Watching that trust grow was astonishing. And, I'll admit, a little humbling. It turns out people don't need you to be an oracle. They need you to stop blocking the door. Over time, I realized something radical. The goal of teaching wasn't to make myself indispensable. It was the opposite. To help people not need me. To fire me, gently and with appreciation. And somehow, instead of threatening my role, this made teaching more alive and far more fun.

Erich describes this as "telling them what to do without telling them what to do." I finally understood what he meant. It's a delicate dance. Fewer strict marching orders, a lot more jazz.

Of course, it wasn't simple. Not everyone felt comfortable being set free, even briefly. Some students were certain they were paying me to tell them exactly what to do, preferably with confidence and certainty. And sometimes, they were right. Part of teaching was learning how to meet people where they were, offering structure when needed and spaciousness when possible.

I also learned that inner listening isn't the same as indulging habit. Sometimes what feels "right" is just familiar. Practice still asks us to hold our patterns up to the light, not to obey them unquestioningly. Curiosity, it turns out, is not the same thing as doing whatever you want.

Unlearning was a return of agency. Over the years, as mistakes accumulated and no one died, something loosened in me. The belief that teachers should be flawless dissolved. Beneath it was a quieter truth: people didn't need me to be perfect. They needed me to be present and preferably awake.

The authority didn't disappear but it sure changed shape, drifting toward becoming relational rather than positional. Responsive rather than prescriptive. Alive rather than memorized.

That made me harder to categorize in a world that prefers clean lineages and tidy labels. By then, I had already unlearned the need to fit. Which, in retrospect, may have been the whole point. I didn't yet realize that the same skills I was learning as a teacher were about to be asked of me in a far more personal way. I didn't know, yet, that unlearning would soon be required of me in ways no class could prepare me for.

10

THE BODY REMEMBERS
WHAT LOVE TAUGHT IT

Grief doesn't ask your permission. It also doesn't behave itself. It wanders in sideways, rearranges things you weren't planning to touch, and leaves the door open so everything else in your life can wander through too.

When my dad died, it wasn't a single collapse or epiphany. It was more like a weather front that moved in slowly, then suddenly, then stalled. Looking back, the surprising part wasn't the grief itself. It was realizing I had already been preparing for it without knowing. For years, I'd been learning how to feel. Not efficiently or gracefully. But persistently. Learning how to breathe into confusion, how to soften around discomfort, how to let sensation teach me what words couldn't.

What grief revealed wasn't something new, but what had already been taught to me through love, and where it lived when I needed it. Montana had taught me that. Yoga had taught me that. And whatever thread had been quietly weaving through my life since childhood had been training me for moments when the world tilts.

One of the first places I felt grief rearrange itself into something else was in my car.

I'd be driving familiar local roads, often on the way to the yoga studio, the kind of roads you've driven so many times you know where every pothole is. Your hands turn the wheel without much thought. Music usually playing. My body already in motion toward something known, something my dad would have politely tolerated rather than chosen.

And there he'd be.

Not in a spooky or dramatic way. More as a felt presence than an apparition, the way someone you've loved for decades can live inside your posture, your timing, your way of listening. He sat in the passenger seat the way he always had at family gatherings, quiet and attentive, taking everything in.

My father wasn't antisocial. He was a listener extraordinaire. He didn't rush conversation or compete with it. He waited, not passively, but with a steady interest that made room for other people to arrive fully.

In those drives, I found myself telling him things the way I always had. About learning a musical instrument and how strange it was to let sound come before understanding. About how odd it felt that people thought he was permanently gone, how that didn't match my experience at all. I told him how the chipper nurse's word, "expired," had landed in me, how wrong it sounded for someone who still moved through my days with such steadiness. It made me think of cartons and labels and dates stamped in ink, not of this warm, unmistakable nearness.

I didn't hear his answers so much as recognize them, already shaped by years of being known. There would be a warmth spreading through me, a quiet certainty. He was there, riding shotgun on roads my body knew by heart.

That season included other parts of my life shaking loose, producing a level of angst so consuming sometimes that it felt like living in a house with faulty wiring. The lights flickered constantly, and no one could find the breaker. Something long-standing and stabilizing, something I'd relied on for decades, was suddenly gone, not by choice or timing, but by force. My nervous system behaved exactly as you'd expect when the ground disappears without warning.

Grief didn't overwhelm me so much as *join the party.* Loudly. But grief, oddly, was the most honest one in the room. It didn't hide behind subtext or disguise itself as productivity or politeness. It arrived saying the one thing that was unmistakably true: you loved him. You were loved back. And this hurts because of that.

My mind struggled to keep up, while my body, smarter than I gave it credit for, was already responding. It trembled when it needed to, sagged into chairs, and took long, involuntary exhales in the middle of the night when sleep refused to cooperate. It knew when to soften and when to hold. My body understood how to metabolize heartbreak long before my mind learned how to think about it.

That was when Erich's words stopped being philosophical and became practical: You are the awareness that is aware of what's happening. I wasn't drowning. I was experiencing.

~

Around the same time, nature, unsentimental and reliable, became my tether in a way it never had before.

Not the inspirational-poster version of nature, but the kind that exists beside you without commentary. One hot afternoon in Montana, I gingerly walked down a muddy embankment toward a small, icy creek, grabbing onto twigs and roots for balance and thanking them under my breath for being there as I intruded. I took off my shoes and plunged my feet into the water.

The cold rushed in like a loving bitch-slap. The creek was not interested in my emotional processing. It didn't care about my grief, my anxiety, or my search for meaning. It shocked me fully into my body, into the undeniable fact of sensation. Apparently, this was the creek's version of compassion.

Right before that moment, I'd been thinking about how much my sensory-aware friends and teachers seemed to understand. Right after, I felt an overwhelming gratitude to be alive on Earth in an Earth suit that included feet. The creek didn't comfort me. It reminded me I was here and I'd be wise to pay attention to that.

Nature spoke in a grammar my body already understood, sometimes abrupt, sometimes soothing, never interested in my interpretation.

Back home, there were other anchors. Dogwoods behind my house that steadied me on mornings when anxiety felt thick. Trails I walked until my thoughts got bored. Sunlight through the windshield that felt like a small, undeserved blessing. A cat landing in my lap at exactly the wrong and right moment, applying pressure like a furry AED.

None of this solved grief. But it accompanied me. Nature didn't soothe so much as co-regulate; a quiet biological intelligence non-human animals seem to understand long before humans try to explain it.

And then there was my mother.

I'd always loved her, but the early years after my dad's death revealed a different register of strength. The kind forged by loving one man for nearly sixty years and waking up each morning committed to continuing. I remember visiting her not long after he died and walking past the bedroom where she was on the phone with her sister, giggling like a kid over some shared childhood memory.

It stopped me in my tracks. She wasn't bypassing grief. She wasn't drowning in it either. She was choosing life in increments: meals to make, people to welcome, sisters to laugh with. Watching her didn't just deepen my love for her. It rewrote it. Love, I realized, doesn't end when someone dies, but it does change tempo.

The clearest proof that the body remembers what love taught it came later, quietly.

During the pandemic, I took up learning the banjo. I learned one song not from sheet music, but by ear and imitation. As I practiced, I noticed something almost embarrassingly specific. My head tilted slightly. My gaze drifted toward nothing in particular. A small smile appeared without my asking it to. My face, apparently, had its own memory.

It was exactly the way my father played the concertina. In that moment, it felt as though he had moved into me, quietly and without announcement. Not as a thought or a recollection, but as a physical way of being. He was there in the angle of my head, in the softening of my eyes, in the timing of my hands. Love arrived not as nostalgia, but as continuity. It was him and it was me, carried forward through posture, gesture, and attention, through the body remembering what the mind never had to hold.

Looking back now, what astonishes me isn't that I endured that season, but that I'm standing in a life I couldn't have imagined from inside it. At the time, I was just trying to get through the day without unraveling completely. The idea that something good, spacious, even joyful might grow out of that terrain would have felt laughable and unrealistic.

And yet here I am, not because I powered through or figured things out, but because something kept moving me forward, inch by inch, even when I couldn't see where I was going. Everything I had learned—movement, stillness, yoga, Montana, nature, my own nervous system—braided itself into an inner ballast. It didn't make the darkness disappear, but it gave me enough moxie to keep going.

There were moments when anxiety grew so loud it sometimes suggested impossible thoughts, which passed as quickly as they arrived and never returned. What stayed was something quieter and more trustworthy. A sense that even when things were filthy and narrow and disorienting, there was still a direction. Still a way through.

Grief didn't make me wise. But it made me a little more honest, more animal, more human. It stripped away the fantasy that I needed to understand everything to survive it.

The body remembers what love taught it long after the mind runs out of explanations. And without my quite realizing it yet, that remembering was no longer just about grief. It had become a form of instruction, one I trusted instinctively, even before I understood how often my body had been leading all along.

11

THE BODY ALREADY KNEW

For most of my life, I treated my body like a cheerful, durable sidekick. Helpful, loyal, mildly dramatic, but not upper management. My brain, meanwhile, was convinced it was CEO. It narrated, strategized, overruled. If my body sent a memo, my brain stamped it Noted and filed it unread.

This arrangement worked well enough for a long time. Until it didn't.

As life unfolded through yoga, nature, Montana, grief, middle age, and an increasing amount of time spent barefoot outdoors, a small realization took shape: my body had been paying attention the entire time. And it was much better at its job than my brain gave it credit for. What surprised me most was that this wasn't just about how I taught yoga. It was about how I lived.

People often talk about embodiment as if it's an advanced spiritual elective. Something you take once your schedule clears and you finally know how to pronounce interoception. But embodiment is far more ordinary than that, and far more radical.

Embodiment is simply living inside yourself with some degree of partnership.

It's noticing the flutter in your stomach before your brain constructs a full backstory. It's sensing your shoulders inching toward your ears and inviting them back down. It's realizing a tight jaw isn't a personality trait. It's data.

Embodiment isn't mystical. But it is physical, and physical is usually honest. I didn't learn this through lofty meditation or moments of exceptional discipline. I learned it in real time, mostly while teaching, often while mildly confused.

There was a stretch when I'd be lightly demonstrating a sequence in class, my carefully written notes nearby, cues drilled into me by teacher trainings past. On paper, everything made sense. But as I moved, my body would suddenly interrupt with a very clear question: why are you doing it this way?

I rarely had a good answer.

Sometimes the interruption was subtle. A pause that wanted to be longer. A transition that felt unnecessarily fussy. Other times it was unmistakable. A firm internal nudge that said, this is not it.

And then, without consulting my notes or my training or whatever imaginary panel of yoga elders I thought was watching, I'd change the instruction on the fly. No script. No safety net. Just sensation and a willingness to trust it.

Here's the surprising part. It worked.

Students didn't look confused or alarmed, but they sure softened. They followed. The room felt more coherent, not less. My body seemed to be saying, with patience, you can feel this. Why are you making it harder than it needs to be? That was when I began to understand that embodiment wasn't something I was teaching. It was something I was finally letting lead.

Online, I saw plenty of messaging that treated movement as performance. Something you execute well or poorly, something to get right. But the older I get, the clearer it becomes. Movement isn't something the body performs. Movement is what the body is.

We humans are animals with complex inner weather. And animals move to regulate state. They stretch, shake, curl, expand. None of it is aesthetic. All of it is functional.

Somatic training later gave language to what my body had known all along. Movement is how the nervous system resets itself. It's our original language. Somewhere along the way, my body developed what I can only describe as opinions. Not dramatic ones. Reliable ones.

A soft lift in my sternum: *yes.*

A constriction in my ribcage: *no.*

Heaviness behind the eyes: *rest, not productivity.*

A restless hum under the skin: *move.* Outside, preferably.

These signals had been there for years. I had been too busy being reasonable to listen. As I trusted sensation more, my teaching shifted again. My cues softened. "Try this," instead of "Do this." "Notice what your breath wants," instead of "Inhale now." "Let the movement arise," instead of "Lift your arm."

I became less of a director and more of a facilitator. Less technician, more friendly co-conspirator. Teaching became more spacious, and honestly, more fun.

The more time I spent outside breathing at the pace of trees, wading creeks, watching horizons, the more obvious it became. We're animals trying to live at a speed our bodies never agreed to. Stress makes more sense when you watch how slowly aspens move. Anxiety makes more sense when you notice how rarely we look at anything farther away than a screen. Fatigue makes more sense when you compare yourself to any non-domesticated creature and realize they nap without guilt.

Embodiment isn't self-improvement. It's relationship with sensation, gravity, and the more-than-human world that surrounds and shapes us. Most of us have felt it at least once. A quiet interior nudge. A subtle yes or no that arrives before explanation. We don't always trust it and so we explain it away. But the body is patient. It keeps sending messages.

And if you ignore them long enough, the body may escalate. It starts gently, with nudges and whispers. But it's not above stronger measures. Occasionally, this includes rerouting your life to Montana, where there are fewer distractions and only crappy cell service. Just enough signal to know you're not in charge anymore.

In the end, embodiment isn't a destination. It's a way of being with yourself that's honest, grounded, and surprisingly ordinary. It doesn't ask you to become someone new. It asks you to remember who's been here all along. Your body already knows.

12

PRACTICES I TRUST

If you spend enough time in the yoga world, you eventually accumulate a small mountain of techniques, methods, lineages, sequences, rituals, breath ratios, and other human inventions designed to coax you into a better relationship with your own life. Some of them are brilliant. Some seem ridiculous. Some require a special cushion and an expensive workshop in the Himalayas.

What I've come to trust, though, are the practices that don't need much from me. The ones that ask almost nothing and give back in steady, quiet ways. The ones that remind me the body is not a philosophical concept but an animal with preferences, instincts, and opinions. The ones that return me to myself without demanding that I become holier, more optimized, or more enlightened than I currently am.

These are the practices that survived every fad, every disappointment, every phase of enthusiastic over-efforting, and even the seasons when I couldn't tell up from down.

They aren't "mine." They're simply the ones that kept working. Here they are, in plain language.

Feeling as a Practice, Not Just a Reaction

Not emotional feeling, though that matters too, but the tactile, sensory intelligence in the body. The kind that notices pressure, temperature, pull, release, orientation. The kind we all had as children before we became top-heavy with ideas.

The practice is simply this: Can I feel what's happening before I try to adjust it? Feeling is information. Feeling is feedback. Feeling is the body's way of saying, "Here's our reality. Please stop overriding it."

When I feel first instead of analyze first, something inside settles and reorganizes. Some truth makes itself known without a single word. I trust this because the body never sugarcoats anything. It's incapable of performance.

The Simplest Breath in the World

I've learned complicated breathing techniques with impressive names. Some require counting. Some require visualization. One suggested imagining light pouring through the crown of my head, which only made me think of scalp sunburns.

But the breath that has carried me through airports, conflict, grief, joy, and the purgatory of a turbulent middle seat is embarrassingly simple: Let the exhale go. Let the inhale come. Feel the raw sensation of each, from start to finish.

That's it. A softening on the exhale. A natural return on the inhale. Two seconds of honesty repeated until something inside you gives up its white-knuckle grip. I trust this breath because it doesn't ask me to manage anything, only to stop interrupting myself.

Move Until Something Makes Sense Again

Some days my entire wellness plan is: wiggle until you can think straight. Cat–cow until the spine stops sounding like popcorn. Neck rolls until your jaw remembers it's allowed to go off duty. A slow side bend that reintroduces you to your ribcage one intercostal at a time.

Movement is orientation, your body pointing gently toward home. Even ninety seconds of honest, pressure-free movement will reorganize what three hours of cognitive effort can't touch. I trust movement because it tells the truth more efficiently than my mind ever has.

Going Outside

Nature doesn't ask us to be spiritual, productive, optimistic, or profound. It doesn't require intention-setting. It simply presents itself: wind, ground, water, sky. Stepping outside, even briefly, recalibrates something in me that no meditation cushion has ever reached.

Cold river water on overheated feet. A breeze slipping through pine needles. A crow giving me side-eye like I'm the least interesting creature it has seen all day. These things restore my animal nature: the earthy, sensory, instinctive part of me that disappears under fluorescent light and responsibility. I trust nature because it expects nothing and still gives everything.

Rhythm (Your Nervous System's Native Language)

After years teaching against the soundtrack of wind in aspen leaves, and years learning rhythm from my friend Matthew, I've realized rhythm is the nervous system's oldest regulator.

Footfalls on a trail. The thrum of a drum. Your own breath whispering in repetition. Rhythm doesn't ask you to understand it; it simply reorganizes what's inside you. I trust rhythm because my body does, instantly and without negotiation.

Choosing the Next Gentle Thing

Forget the "right" thing. Forget the "high vibration" thing. Forget the productivity-friendly thing. The next gentle thing is always enough: A sip of water. A shoulder drop. One honest breath. A six-second stretch. A softer tone with myself.

It's not dramatic, but it's a quiet compass. It says, "This way. Slowly. Kindly." I trust it because it almost never fails to bring me back into myself.

Music (and the Banjo, Against All Odds)

There's one more practice I trust, though it still surprises me to admit it: music. Or more specifically, the banjo. I picked it up at the very start of the pandemic because nothing guarantees social distancing like a beginner banjo player. Instant perimeter.

I am not musically gifted. I don't practice consistently. I learn slowly and forget quickly. And yet the banjo has a way of settling me that feels borderline miraculous. A few sloppy rolls, a gentle brush of the thumb, and my nervous system does this tiny sigh, like, Oh right, this.

It's not about getting better. My banjo teacher Braeden says music isn't something you master; it's something you join. That feels true. When I'm picking away—not well, but earnestly—something in me arranges itself. The rhythm works on me the way trails and creeks do, reminding my body that it belongs to a larger pulse.

So yes, I trust the banjo. Not because I'm good at it (I'm objectively not), but because it brings me back to sensation, to play, to aliveness. Which, come to think of it, is all any good practice ever does.

These practices—the simple ones, the elemental ones, including trembling knees, honest movement, and the unlikely magic of a badly played banjo—don't demand mastery. They require noticing, presence, and willingness to stop talking over yourself.

I've come to trust that the thread doesn't just pull us toward what's true for us, but it also keeps widening our field of concern. Following it hasn't made me more certain, but it's made me more aware that everyone is navigating something unseen. And that makes me more willing to meet people where they are.

Finally, the practices can offer a way of coming home to yourself without climbing any spiritual ladders. And here's the part I think I trust the most: *things reorganize when they are witnessed.* Bodies soften when they feel attended to. Life gets clearer when you stop drowning it in commentary.

13

PEOPLE HELP ME HAPPEN

I used to think my path was shaped mostly by instincts, accidents, and the occasional strong nudge from whatever invisible hand I've been calling "the thread." And that's partly true. It's probably why I walked into yoga sideways and why my compass has always pointed toward teachers who handed the steering wheel back to me with a soft, "Take it for a spin, see what you find." But the longer I live, the harder it is to ignore another truth running alongside it: I didn't get here alone. For someone with a lifelong suspicion of authority, that took a while to admit.

But here's the part I don't want to gloss over: Despite all my suspicions about certainty, I have been shaped, profoundly, by other people. Not in the "they knew better than me" way. More in the "thank God I didn't have to evolve alone" way.

There's something downright miraculous about how guidance works when it's not imposed. How teachers, friends, coworkers, strangers on airplanes, the soft-spoken person in the back row, end up shaping you simply by living near your life. Erich shaped me, of course. Not through charisma or prescriptions, but through presence, through listening, through giving me back to myself.

But he's not the only one. Not by a long shot.

I've been shaped by the friend who told me to "drop fear" while I was spiraling in the Milwaukee airport. Shaped by a coworker who once said, "Just do the next sensible thing," at a time when I was hoping for a burning bush. Shaped by students whose honest, bewildered faces taught me more about humility than any manual.

Shaped by strangers whose kindness left dents. Shaped, unexpectedly, by people who irritated me into clarity. And shaped, though I don't want to give them more oxygen than they deserve, by the ones who hurt me. Not because the hurt was noble or necessary, but because it forced me to choose: shrink or grow, collapse or reorient, numb or feel. There were seasons when I believed the only wisdom worth trusting was the kind that arrived through mystical experiences, profound insights, Montana mornings with ravens dropping things like cosmic punctuation marks.

And yet, more often than not, what steadied me was... people. Not their answers, but their willingness to stay. Their patience, their timing, and their offhand comments that landed like breadcrumbs on the path. Their mistakes, which taught me what not to emulate. Their generosity, which taught me I didn't have to do it all alone. Most consistently, that steadiness came from my husband, who never needed my path to make sense to support it, and who has somehow managed to keep my happiness high on his list even when I kept rearranging the map.

One of the things I've learned from the people who shaped me is that compassion spreads less through instruction than through proximity. Spend enough time around people who take others seriously, who assume dignity even under pressure, who move toward service without making a production of it, and something in you quietly recalibrates. You listen differently. You pause longer. You offer help without first rehearsing a thoughtful, articulate, entirely unnecessary speech in your head.

I've been deeply influenced by Tibetan teachings, not because they urge compassion, but because they assume it. As if caring for others isn't a virtue so much as the natural consequence of seeing clearly. When suffering is understood as universal, kindness stops being heroic and starts being practical.

It took me decades to understand that being shaped by others doesn't require surrendering sovereignty. It's more like being in a long, evolving apprenticeship to the human condition. We're all borrowing wisdom from one another, passing it along, misquoting it, refining it, laughing about it, reinventing it, losing it, remembering it.

Every insight I've ever had, every "thread," every moment of recognition, every quiet opening, has had fingerprints on it. Sometimes obvious ones. Sometimes subtle ones, like the woman who fell out of table pose. Sometimes anonymous ones, like the acquaintance whose simple kindness reminded me that I wasn't, in fact, falling off the edge of the earth.

And yes, sometimes the shaping came from people who knocked my life sideways. I'm not saintly enough to pretend I'm grateful for the delivery method. But I can say, without melodrama, that I'm grateful for what unfolded afterward: the new community, the new work, the aliveness I found because something cracked.

So here's the truth I never imagined writing when I was younger: I am suspicious of authoritarian certainty, but I am not self-made. None of us are. We are braided together by influence, by care, by timing, by shared bewilderment, by the invisible generosity of everyone who leaves a trace on us whether they know it or not.

And, gently, may I ask you too: Who helped shape the person reading these words right now? Whose voice or presence still lives in your gestures, your decisions, your courage? You don't need to name them aloud. Just feel for the thread. It may be thinner than you think, but I doubt it's accidental. So often we're helping each other happen without knowing it. A sentence said in passing. A pause where someone didn't rush you. A hand on your back when you didn't ask for one. These moments rarely announce themselves as important. But they accumulate and they can alter trajectories.

14

ONGOING APPRENTICESHIP IN BEGINNING AGAIN

I used to hope there would come a time in my life when I'd finally know what I was doing, when I'd stop fumbling and second-guessing and drafting my way through each new stage like the world's oldest intern. I imagined that adulthood, if done correctly, would eventually hand me a certificate of competence.

It hasn't so far.

What it's handed me instead is a long series of beginnings. Some chosen. Some accidental. And one so consuming that it still resists language on the page. All I can say is that it rearranged me down to the studs and then asked me to keep going anyway. It tested the far edges of my capacity to cope. There were long stretches when getting through meant one breath at a time, holding tight to a thread I trusted more out of hope and habit than certainty, and sometimes wondering if I was clutching air.

I didn't ask for that initiation. I didn't want it. And yet, in a sideways and still suspicious way, I'm grateful for it. A small, persistent voice in me asks whether it had to unfold quite like that. But still, when I look at the life that emerged afterward, the people who found me, the community that blossomed, and the work that became possible only because something big cracked open, I can't bring myself to wish it away. I don't like imagining who I'd be without it.

I wouldn't tell my younger self any of this, of course. She wouldn't have had the patience to hear it. She was far too busy trying to prevent catastrophe by being perfect.

She learned early, like so many of us do, that competence earns safety, clarity earns approval, and certainty earns belonging. But none of that turned out to be true. What happened is that every major turning point in my life arrived disguised as a beginning: something awkward, unpolished, and often wildly inconvenient.

Even my professional non-yoga working life trained me for this. I've had real-world jobs where I showed up on the first day with a new key card, a new email address, and not a single clue what I was supposed to be doing. I took notes, nodded like I understood the acronyms, and then went home and Googled half the vocabulary I'd pretended to recognize.

Eventually, I learned the only reliable strategy: show up sincerely, keep your eyes open, ask real questions when you must, and trust that the chips will land where they land. It turned out that "doing my damn best" was not a fallback plan but a perfectly functional operating system.

Teaching yoga wasn't all that different. Being on the mat with students, trying to offer cues without pretending

I was the boss of their bodies, taught me that beginning again wasn't something you got over. It was a state of being. The more honest I became about not knowing everything, the more trustworthy I became as a teacher. Humility wasn't a flaw in my methodology; it was my methodology.

That's the thing no one tells you when you're chasing certainty: beginnings aren't a mark of inadequacy. They're a sign you're still alive, still willing, still in motion.

There's a reason the natural world doesn't seem to reward anyone for looking competent. Rivers don't try to perfect their technique. Trees don't agonize about whether they should be blooming earlier in the season. They begin again, quite literally, every single year. They waste no energy pretending they're further along than they are.

Nature's logic is: start where you are. And if that fails: start again. Some of my most meaningful insights didn't arrive when I was striving for mastery but when I was quietly unraveling. When something in me was forced to soften because the usual strategies stopped working. Those were the seasons that taught me the most enduring lesson of all: beginnings are not the opposite of wisdom. They're its apprenticeship.

If anything in this humble little book has a secret engine, this is it. We are never done with beginnings. We return to them like tides. We cycle through them the way forests shed and regrow. Beginning again is not a failure of progress; it's the rhythm of being and becoming human animals.

So instead of seeking transcendence or mastery or whatever shiny finish line I once thought existed, I'm learning to trust a gentler arrangement: feel what's real, follow what softens, and bow to the wisdom of starting over, again and again, with humor when possible and grace when available.

Which brings me to you. If you've ever found yourself at the edge of a new beginning, wanted or unwanted, wondering if you're late, or behind, or unprepared, please hear this in the softest possible voice: you're right on time. If something in your life is dissolving, rerouting, or changing shape, it doesn't mean you mismanaged anything. It means you're participating in the same ancient rhythm everything in nature obeys. And if you're in one of those seasons now, the kind where you're holding the thread but not quite sure where it's leading? Welcome. You're in excellent company. None of us ever graduate from the apprenticeship of beginning.

15
____

WHAT I THINK I KNOW NOW
THAT I DIDN'T KNOW THEN

If I could tap my younger self on the shoulder, the one anxiously flipping through *Yoga Journal*, or pacing the Milwaukee airport, or whispering prayers in a tipi under the Montana sky, I wouldn't tell her to "be brave" or "trust the process." She wouldn't have believed me anyway.

What I would say is something simpler, something it took me decades to understand: you don't need to know as much as you think you do. You only need to feel what's happening. The revelations that reorganize your life don't come from certainty. They come from sensation and presence. From the willingness to stop narrating your experience long enough to have one.

Here's what else I know now, thanks to yoga, Montana, heartbreak, aging, and the occasional raven dropping a pinecone at my feet as if to say, "Get over yourself." None of this is fancy.

*Your body can be wiser than
your most polished ideology.*

I spent years assuming I needed better beliefs, more teachers, fresh frameworks, some elegant latticework of insight that would at last settle everything inside me. Instead, what settled me was learning what my own ribs feel like when I exhale, what my feet feel like on pine needles, or how my back softens when I stop holding myself upright by sheer force of will.

The body knows things directly, not metaphorically. It speaks in pressure, warmth, fatigue, opening, tightness, buzzing, settling. When I began to trust those messages, life stopped feeling like a riddle. **Have you ever noticed a moment when your body knew the truth before your mind caught up?** A tightening, a softening, a quiet inner "no," or an effortless "yes"? You don't have to call it intuition. You don't have to make it mystical. It's nothing more than your system telling the truth.

*People who seem certain are often
pretending, and that's none of my business.*

I've learned there's no prize for arguing with someone who's built an identity out of being right. I don't need to correct them, convert them, or rescue their humility. Their certainty doesn't have to become my problem. It's information: useful for deciding where not to place my blind trust, my envy, or my energy.

The people I trust most are the ones who live in

ongoing inquiry. They're the ones who say things like, "Hmm... let me feel into that," or "I'm not sure yet," or "Ask me tomorrow." They're not performing doubt; they're practicing honesty. Meanwhile, the people who are certain? They make me want to grab my coat and remember a sudden, urgent appointment elsewhere.

Humility doesn't make you small but it does keep you open and human. And it keeps you close to what's real.

There's no such thing as being "behind."

I started yoga in my forties. I learned how to listen inward in my fifties. I learned how to trust my body after hip surgery in my sixties. And I'm still learning not to panic when the toothpaste runs out. Time is not a racecourse. Healing is not on a semester schedule. And your life does not follow anyone's syllabus, least of all the spiritual-industrial complex. What matters is responsiveness, not speed. Sincerity, not performance. Presence, not impressiveness.

Nature teaches better than any philosophy book.

I've read sublime texts about embodiment, consciousness, mysticism, and neurobiology. They were wonderful. But nothing has taught me more than plunging my body into a cold lake on a hot day or the wind rearranging my thoughts without asking. Or a deer holding my gaze long enough to make it clear that all my spiritual over-complication was unnecessary because there was nothing to decode and nothing hiding behind the moment. Only the moment itself, fully sufficient.

Nature doesn't lecture, require belief, or ask you to fill out an evaluation form. It shows you how things are and invites you back into your animal, actual life.

Insight arrives when you stop chasing it.

I used to think I needed to hunt down understanding: meditate harder, analyze more, journal until the pen begged for mercy. Now I know insight behaves like wildlife: the more you crash around trying to spot it, the farther it slips away. But if you go still—feel, breathe, soften—it wanders over. Curious and unhurried. Once, carrying a pinecone, as if to say, "Let's not get dramatic."

The most reliable way to meet truth is to stop forcing introductions.

The thread is real.

That quiet inner tug, the one that says, "this way," is not wishful thinking or delusion. It's guidance in its most unassuming form, a kind of inner gravity pulling you toward what's already yours. Not fate or prophecy but a kind of coherence, a way your life recognizes itself.

When I've followed it, my world has widened in ways I couldn't have strategized. When I've ignored it, everything tightened, as if I were trying to live inside shoes that are two sizes too small. The thread has never raised its voice. It has only whispered. But over the years, I've learned the shape of its whisper, the way it catches in my ribs, the way the body nods before the mind catches up. I'm not always perfect at listening, but I am getting a little better at turning toward it.

You don't permanently lose the people you love.

I used to dread death with an intensity that sat in my stomach like a sunken stone. Not in the abstract, in the intimate. My parents aging terrified me. Hospitals terrified me. The idea of losing someone I loved felt unendurable.

And yes, death still spooks me. I tense up when the radiologist says, "We'd like a few more images." My chest tightens when a friend gets a scary diagnosis. I fell apart into a thousand pieces when my friend Carie died. Watching my husband age alongside me is its own subtle existential ache.

None of that has evaporated, but something has grown underneath it. When my dad died, something happened that neither my childhood nor most of my adulthood had prepared me for. I didn't lose him. The form changed. The address changed. But the connection held. I remember the room being very still, the soft, metronomic pulse of the monitor, the weight of his hand in mine. The golden thread from childhood to that bedside, and beyond it, did not fray.

When I tried to speak about it later, a few well-meaning friends urged caution. They worried that I might be shielding myself from the worst grief by believing something had happened that maybe hadn't. I heard the care underneath their concern. But what happened wasn't something I decided to believe. It arrived whole and unmistakable, leaving a mark that time hasn't thinned in seventeen years.

I don't pretend to understand the metaphysics, but I know what it felt like and it sure didn't feel like erasure. It felt like steady, familiar continuity. Fear still visits me, but now it has something softer to land on.

Embodiment is not a technique; it's a reunion.

No one can teach you how to come home to your body. They can guide, suggest, and model but the reunion itself is ordinary, private, and personal. Embodiment isn't enlightened posture, but it is noticing your jaw unclench, feeling your feet, loosening your belly, remembering you have a spine, letting gravity hold you instead of effort.

It's intimate, not mystical. And it's available in every moment you're willing to feel rather than perform.

Relief tells you something.

This may be the most surprising lesson of all: the things that make you exhale are not random. They are directional. Relief is the body's way of saying, *Yes. Here. This. More of this.*

We spend a lot of time listening to urgency, obligation, and the loud inner committee that insists everything important must feel hard. Relief arrives differently and without shouting. It loosens your shoulders. It drops your tongue from the roof of your mouth. It makes you realize you have been holding your breath for longer than you care to admit.

Relief is wisdom in disguise. Intuition incarnate. A quiet truth knocking on the inside of your ribs, not demanding certainty, only asking for a little trust. It rarely comes with a five-year plan or a laminated roadmap. It only says, this way feels truer than that way.

If you follow relief, not as an escape hatch but as a compass, I doubt you will lose your way. You may move more slowly, and you may surprise yourself. You may even disappoint the part of you that equates suffering with virtue. But you will be pointed toward something real.

The point of all this isn't transcending ordinary life, it's intimacy with it.

I used to think yoga was about rising above, becoming lighter, loftier, better. What I know now is that the whole trip is about becoming more here: more present and available to your own life. Not elevated, but integrated. And maybe that's the distilled essence of everything I've learned so far: feel what's real, follow what softens, trust what's steady, and let your actual, ordinary, miraculous life be the teacher.

Before you go thinking this is some mystical skill set everyone else has mastered, let me reassure you: you're already doing it. If even one of these ideas lands in your own body as a tiny "oh . . . yes," then this little book will have done its job.

~

Following the Thread. *By now, I don't expect things to resolve. The thread was never leading me toward clarity or a clean ending. It doesn't wrap anything up. It doesn't trade attention for certainty. It asks me to notice when I've stopped paying attention at all.*

And I still lose it. Often. Usually in ordinary ways, by rushing, overthinking, trying to get it right. The familiar distractions. Nothing dramatic. What's changed is that getting lost no longer feels like failure. It feels like information. A signal that I've drifted into habit and away from what's happening in real time.

The thread doesn't correct me but doesn't congratulate me either. It shows up in the same places it always has in the body when something tightens or releases, in the moment I realize I'm holding my breath for no good reason, in the small relief of telling the truth quietly and without decoration.

I don't follow it because it leads somewhere impressive. I follow it because when I don't, things start to feel slightly off, like a room where the air has gone stale. So this is where I am, still circling. Still paying attention when I remember to. Not finished or fixed, but just more willing to begin again from wherever I am. That's as far as the thread goes. For now.

16

THE THREAD, TODAY

Folks talk about "coming full circle" as though life were tidy enough to cooperate. Mine hasn't been. I'm not sure anyone's has.

What I'm describing here isn't a revelation, or a breakthrough, or anything I'd recommend aspiring to. It may simply be what happens when a person stays alive long enough to recognize their own patterns of aliveness. The things that keep resurfacing. The places attention naturally lands. The moments that feel quietly right without offering proof.

Over time, those repetitions begin to feel less like coincidence and more like the sheer miracle of ongoingness. What I've called a "thread" may be nothing more mystical than learning to stop ignoring something we all live with and realizing how freaking sacred it is.

It no longer feels like a mystical flare fired from the heavens. It's more like an internal compass you forget about until you realize you've been navigating by it for years.

These days it shows up in small, throwaway moments. The beat before I teach—fiddling with the thermostat, refolding a blanket—when that familiar inner spaciousness unspools, a breath I didn't take on purpose. Or when I stand near a massive tree and my whole body responds as though I'm being remembered by something ancient. Or when late-winter light glances off the kitchen window and something in me murmurs, Yes. This. Stay for a spell.

I'm still human, still anxious, still prone to spirals of Olympic caliber. I still Google symptoms at 2 a.m., which is self-harm disguised as research. But woven through all that is an undercurrent of recognition, as if life has been whispering the same message for decades and I'm at last starting to lean in.

The thread is clearest when I teach, not in the fancy cues or the sequence or the poem I debated cutting, but in the quiet between things. The exhale after a transition. The shared stillness in *savasana*. The moment someone stops "doing yoga" and starts experiencing themselves.

That's where the thread hums: in the softening, the unbracing, the small acts of permission people grant themselves when no one is demanding perfection.

Nature, meanwhile, continues to do what nature does: recalibrate me without fanfare. Trails redraw my interior geography. Rivers rewrite the static in my system and a forest reminds me I am far more animal, and far more trustworthy, than any grand philosophy ever suggested.

The body is a way of knowing. Not as metaphor, but as fact. The more I live inside that intelligence, the less I need certainty and the more I value direction. The thread isn't a destination. It's a pull that's steady and persistent. I don't follow it every time, but I follow it more often. That may be as close as most of us come to clarity.

And now, if you'll allow me, I want to turn toward you once more. If you've stayed with me this far, please know I don't take that lightly. Attention is a rare mineral these days, and you spent some of yours wandering with me through whatever shines beneath the floorboards of an ordinary life.

Have you ever felt a tug like this? A shimmer of rightness you couldn't justify but also couldn't ignore? If so, you don't need to name it or elevate it or turn it into a spiritual project or side hustle. Just recognize it. Threads don't require belief; they do request a little cooperation. Even small, clumsy cooperation counts.

If you haven't felt anything like that, or aren't sure, that's okay too. Threads have patience. They tug when they tug. They find us when we're ready, or when we're too tired to resist. I didn't arrive anywhere in this life through wisdom. I arrived through willingness that was sometimes reluctant, sometimes ungraceful, sometimes propelled forward like a kid nudged onto a school stage by a well-meaning parent.

I don't pretend to understand the afterlife or consciousness or why ravens drop pinecones at poetic moments. I don't know whether the thread is destiny, intuition, biology, imagination, or a cosmic prank with good timing. I do know that life feels far less random and far more participatory than I once believed.

I know what it feels like. And feeling, at this point, has become a steadier teacher than certainty ever was. I know that people we love don't disappear; they change form. I know that nature speaks to anyone who slows down enough to listen. I know that the body tells the truth with more consistency than the mind.

And I know that whatever intelligence breathes through this world—call it God, consciousness, the Mystery, or life being life—has a sense of humor. I've seen the timing. I've seen the coincidences. I've seen the Crocs.

If this little book has done anything, I hope it reminded you of some quiet instinct or remembered belonging that predates the noise. Maybe it's a place, a breath, a teacher. Maybe it's the tug of your own thread, steady and patient.

Whatever it is, may you follow it in your own imperfect way. And if our threads cross in a studio, on a trail, in Montana, or in the fluorescent aisle of a grocery store where potato chips are on sale, I hope we recognize each other not by certainty, but by curiosity. The oh, you too of wandering humans.

Whatever thread you're following, luminous or stubborn, travels better with a sense of humor. Keep yours close. You're going to need it.

If you have a thread, and I suspect you were issued one at birth, may it keep brushing your awareness, tugging at you in ways you can't quite explain but also can't ignore. And may you follow it, not because you're certain, but because some old, wordless part of you rises to meet it.

ACKNOWLEDGMENTS

This little book, like most of the better things in my life, exists because of the people who hold me together, crack me open, keep me honest, make me laugh, and remind me that living a human life is not a solo sport.

First, to Bob, who has supported every one of my eccentric and head-scratching endeavors with the steady devotion of someone who puts my contentment above virtually everything, even when he's not entirely sure what I'm doing or why. Your faith has been the ground beneath every risk I've ever taken. Thank you for loving me in all my forms: the reasonable ones, the questionable ones, and the ones held together with duct tape.

To my mom, whose unwavering and overgenerous belief in me sometimes bordered on mistaken identity. She raised five children, maintained a home in near-sacred order, and showed, through raucous laughing fits with her sisters, how community can hold us when nothing else can.

And to my dad, whose calm kindness and music shaped me long before I understood the nature of endings. He taught me, without ever trying, that death is more illusion than fact, and that a life continues to sound its notes long after the last measure.

Thank you both for my siblings: Jim, who set off for the Peace Corps in deepest Africa before most small-town boys had ever left the county; Wayne, the irrepressible jokester with his built-in laugh track; Mary, my irreplaceable sister with a compassionate heart of gold; and Frank, namesake of my cat and an environmental lawyer with so much fire that every case he touches strains toward a Frank Capra ending.

To Erich Schiffmann, whose teachings rearranged my inner architecture so completely that I shudder to imagine who I'd be without his guidance and friendship. Thank you for opening the doorway into presence, listening, and what I can only call aliveness.

To my local yoga gal-pal sangha, Alex, Annie, Andrea, Carol, and Jackie, thank you for the brave, tender, irreverent circle of truth-telling and soul-baring that has carried me through more seasons than I can count. And to Lisa, Margaret, Melissa, Smiley, and Terri, another constellation entirely, my personal wisdom council and emotional emergency response team. Thank you for every conversation, every laugh, every rescue.

To the entire Feathered Pipe family. By "family," I mean the whole entangled web of teachers, staff, students, volunteers, alumni, musicians, cooks, cleaners, wanderers, and dreamers who have circled that pond for five decades. You have shaped my life in ways too numerous to name.

A special bow to Crystal Water, without whom the Feathered Pipe might not exist in the thriving way it does now, and who remains one of my favorite partners-in-crime in stewarding that improbable, feral hippie dream.

To Zane Williams and Matthew Marsolek, two deeply talented humans I'm lucky to know because of the Feathered Pipe, the place where so many of the best things in my life took root. Zane's early guidance helped shape The Mindful Unplug retreat, and his gift for teaching light, as presence, as texture, as revelation, changed not only how I see the world, but how I inhabit it. His sensory-awareness practices seeded some of the retreat's most enduring foundations, and their echoes return each year like familiar music.

Alongside him, Matthew, together with his extraordinary family, has given the retreat one of its truest voices through rhythm, song, story, and heart. Every summer is infused with the kind of joy that resets a room faster than his signature call of "Ba-da-boom!" to which the only correct response, of course, is "Ba-da-bing!" The Marsolek family's wholehearted generosity continues to give the program a depth and aliveness no syllabus could ever replicate.

To four-legged Frank, my citrine-eyed feline roommate, who supervised this writing with his signature blend of indifference, judgment, hand nips, and impeccable timing.

And to you, the brave human who opened this book and offered the astonishing gift of your attention in a world so stingy with quiet. Thank you for your curiosity. Thank you for letting these words meet you wherever you are.

ABOUT THE AUTHOR

Anne Jablonski has spent a little over two decades helping people breathe, move, and stop treating their bodies like unruly coworkers they must manage. A yoga and somatic movement educator, she blends the intuitive, "listen first" approach of Freedom Yoga with the gentle, pattern-unwinding principles of *Movingness*—both of which reassure her daily that the body is far wiser than the anxious, overachieving narrator living in our heads.

She teaches with a mix of tenderness and irreverence, offering students permission to be curious, confused, glorious, imperfect, and ridiculous, often in the same breath. Her approach assumes that self-help isn't about repairing a broken machine; it's about befriending a very alive, very opinionated human ecology. Preferably without pretending to be a finished product.

Anne holds the usual alphabet-soup yoga and somatic movement credentials—including E-RYT® 500, YACEP®, ISMETA ASMP, and American Yoga Council (AYC) Level 3 Teacher—but considers curiosity her truest lineage. She lives in Virginia with her husband, Bob, and Frank the cat, a former street philosopher who supervises her writing with a blend of detachment and grudging affection.

Off the mat, Anne serves on the board of the nonprofit Feathered Pipe Foundation, where she helps a marvelous team to steward a magical and quirky retreat center in Montana that has shaped her life in ways too honest and far too wild for bullet points.

www.ingramcontent.com/pod-product-compliance
Lightning Source LLC
Chambersburg PA
CBHW071447130726
47997CB00006B/2259